1979

Art of Anci

Art of Ancient
CYPRUS

Museum of Fine Arts   Boston   1972

Cover: **12. Amphoroid Krater**   Cypro-Mycenaean Pictorial Style. Late Cypriote II.
Frontispiece: **21. Jar with Loop-Legs**   Bichrome IV Ware. Cypro-archaic I – II.

Copyright © 1972 by the Museum of Fine Arts, Boston, Massachusetts
All rights reserved
Library of Congress Catalogue Card No.: 72–83722
ISBN: 0–87846–068–3

Typeset in Linofilm Palatino by Wrightson Typographers, Boston
Printed in the U.S.A.
by Scroll Press, Danbury, Connecticut

Preface

This catalogue illustrates the best works of ancient art which come directly or ultimately from the island of Cyprus, in the permanent collections of the Museum of Fine Arts, Boston. Most of these items were purchased by subscription from General Luigi Palma di Cesnola on 15 May 1872,* making them among the first Cypriote antiquities to find a home in a major institution in the Western Hemisphere. Others in the collection, but not illustrated here, were given by the Egypt Exploration Fund in 1886 and 1888, as the result of excavations principally at Naukratis in the Nile Delta. A few additions have been made by random gift down to the 1970s. All these works of art are scheduled for exhibition precisely a century, almost to the day, after the purchase from General Cesnola, which marked the first major acquisition by the newly constituted Museum of Fine Arts, Boston. A number of them have been scarcely seen, save by specialists, since the museum was moved from Copley Square to its present home on Huntington Avenue.

This catalogue is the collective work of all members of the Department of Classical Art, regular staff and volunteers, during the past several years. Those responsible include Claire Blackwell, Mary Comstock, Elizabeth Foote, Mary Hollinshead, Juliet Shelmerdine, Penelope Truitt, Emily Vermeule, and myself. The photographs are the work of Claire Blackwell and Herbert Hamilton, Wayne Lemmon, and past members of the museum's photography department. Barbara Hawley, Carl F. Zahn, Ellen F. Farrow, and the Office of Publications are responsible for producing the book.

During the period of preparation, the Department of Classical Art has been deeply involved in all aspects of the Harvard University–Museum of Fine Arts Archaeological Mission in the Morphou area of northwest Cyprus, working under the auspices of the Department of Antiquities, Republic of Cyprus. Many individuals and several organizations have supported this enterprise, chiefly the excavation of the Bronze Age city-sanctuary-tomb(s) at *Toumba Tou Skourou* just north of Morphou. This catalogue is designed to relate the museum's traditional collections to the objects unearthed by excavation here and elsewhere throughout Cyprus in recent years, those works of art so handsomely shown in the Cyprus Museum, Nicosia, and the district museums of the island.

*The exceptions are duly noted.

With these thoughts in mind, it is a distinct pleasure to dedicate this book to the director, officers, and staff of the Department of Antiquities, Republic of Cyprus, and to the curators and staff of the Cyprus Museum, Nicosia.

Dr. and Mrs. Ernest Kahn of Cambridge, Massachusetts, have underwritten the basic cost of this catalogue, making it a permanent record of an aspect of the Museum of Fine Arts which reflects their own field work in the Middle East and in Southeast Asia.

Cornelius Vermeule
Curator, Department of Classical Art

Chronology of Cyprus[*]

5800–4950 B.C.   Neolithic I

5800–3000   For information about earlier periods one should consider the random nature of excavations — much information comes from cemeteries only.

5800–5250   Khirokitia, major settlement near south coast: without metal, with beehive shaped dwellings, stone vessels.

5250–4950   Troulli, on coast east of Kyrenia: pottery in its later phases of occupation: red lustrous and red-on-white.

4950–3500   This chronological gap awaits the evidence of future excavation. A natural calamity may have left Cyprus sparsely inhabited.

3500–3000   Neolithic II

Kalavasos and Sotira, east and west of Limassol: "combed ware" pottery with shiny surface and bands made by a comblike tool in the wet paint; also red-on-white ware. / Obsidian imported from Anatolia in the Neolithic period.

3000–2500   Chalcolithic I Age

Erimi, a major settlement just west of Limassol: red-on-white pottery with geometric or floral patterns applied in bright paint, also red lustrous, black lustrous, and other wares. Copper appears. / Pottery styles suggest contacts with the Syrian-Palestinian coast.

*This chronology is based on P. Dikaios, *A Guide to the Cyprus Museum* (Nicosia, 1961), 3rd rev. ed.

A separate chronology for pottery appears on page 8.

2500–2300   Chalcolithic II Age

Ambelikou, south of Soli: red-on-white ware, also red polished, red-and-black ware, mostly bowls. No evidence of Western Anatolian pottery, such as beak-spouted jugs.

2300   Major upheaval of some nature, also affecting Anatolia and, perhaps, the Syrian coast near Cyprus.

2300–2000 or 1800   Early Bronze Age

Arrival of new civilization, presumably from western Anatolia. Pottery from mainland. Cyprus develops as a copper producing country. / Cemetery at Khrysiliou, northeast of Morphou, contains both western Anatolian (type) and traditional Cypriote vases. / Cypriote potters gradually develop new repertory, using Anatolian shapes and local forms. Bridge-spouted jar indicates connections with metallurgy. / Minoan daggers imported from Crete (Lapethos).

2000 or 1800–1600   Middle Bronze Age

Copper mining increases, with silver and gold more common. / Bronze, not copper, now used for weapons, implements, tools, utensils, and so on. / Red polished pottery of Early Bronze Age replaced by painted ware, with Syrian influence (red-on-white ground).

1800–1700   Minoan goblet found in a tomb near Karmi, inland from Kyrenia. / Trade with Syria and Palestine.

1700–1600   Migrations and movements lead the Hyksos from Asia Minor to Egypt, affecting Cyprus and especially its trade (in the eastern part of the island).

1600–1050 Late Bronze Age

Use of Cypriote-Minoan script, as yet not fully deciphered.

1550	Enkomi (Alasia ?) becomes prominent as copper working center. Site at *Toumba tou Skourou* ("Mound of Blackness") becomes an important copper processing city-sanctuary.
1504–1450	Egyptian Pharaoh Tuthmosis III controls Cyprus, which becomes extremely prosperous (and peaceful).
1400–1200	Influx of Mycenaean peoples from Aegean world to Cyprus; much Mycenaean pottery in Cyprus. The copper working center, Enkomi, near its successor Salamis, becomes a rich city: gold, gems, ivories, scarabs, copper figures, and pottery.
1372–1355	Tablets from the new city at Tell el Amarna, founded by Egyptian Pharaoh Akhenaten, indicate Cyprus sends copper to Egypt as tribute.
1288	Hittites and Egyptians fight the Battle of Kadesh in Syria. Egyptian influence still paramount in Cyprus, but island open to trade and immigration from Aegean as before.
1200–1050	End of Late Bronze Age. Enkomi destroyed in the general upheaval caused by invasions from the north. A new town is built by Achaean colonists traditionally led by Teucer, one of the heroes of the Trojan War. Achaeans also found Kition. / Sea Peoples, defeated by Rameses III (1198–1167), destroy new Enkomi, which is rebuilt by the Achaeans.
1100	New wave of Achaeans, coming from Greece by way of Pamphylia, bring their language, religion, and customs to Cyprus.

1050–700 Geometric Age

1000	Cyprus loses contact with the West because of troubled times and migrations in Greece but communication continues with Syria and Egypt. / Iron substituted for bronze in tools and weapons. / Pottery now wheel-made, with geometric ornament. / In spite of abundance of archaeological evidence, especially pottery, historical events of period are unclear.
900–800	Greek cities and small kingdoms founded in Cyprus. / Phoenician cities and small kingdoms also founded. / Fusion of Cypriote-Mycenaean elements with Syro-Palestinian features gives way to a local, Cypriote pottery, with black-on-red introduced (bichrome). / Phoenician temple built at Kition. Sanctuary of Apollo at Kourion established and continues until fourth century A.D.
800 on	Assyrians conquer Phoenicia and then Egypt. Century of greatest Phoenician colonization and expansion in Cyprus.
750–709	Commercial and maritime prosperity of Cypriote cities. / "Royal" tombs of Salamis. / Near Eastern colonies established by Greeks from the Cyclades and especially Eretria.
709	Cyprus dominated by Assyrians for about fifty years, seven Cypriote kings paying homage to Sargon II.

700–475 Archaic Age

Cyprus has contacts with Archaic Greece, and a good Greek Archaic style develops in sculpture. East Greek pottery brought to Cyprus; Cypriote pottery exported to Rhodes and sculpture to Naukratis.

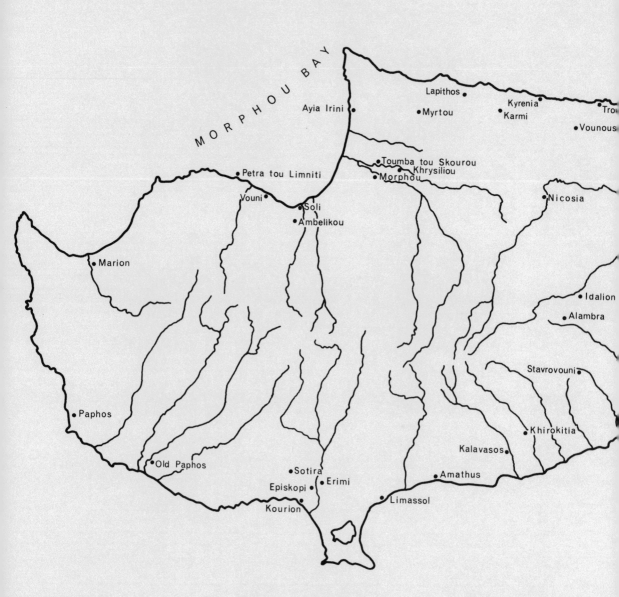

M E D I T E R R A N E A

MORPHOU BAY

Lapithos
Kyrenia
Karmi
Tro
Myrtou
Ayia Irini
Vounous
Toumba tou Skourou
Khrysiliou
Petra tou Limniti
Morphou
Nicosia
Vouni
Soli
Ambelikou
Marion
Idalion
Alambra
Stavrovouni
Paphos
Khirokitia
Kalavasos
Old Paphos
Sotira
Amathus
Erimi
Episkopi
Limassol
Kourion

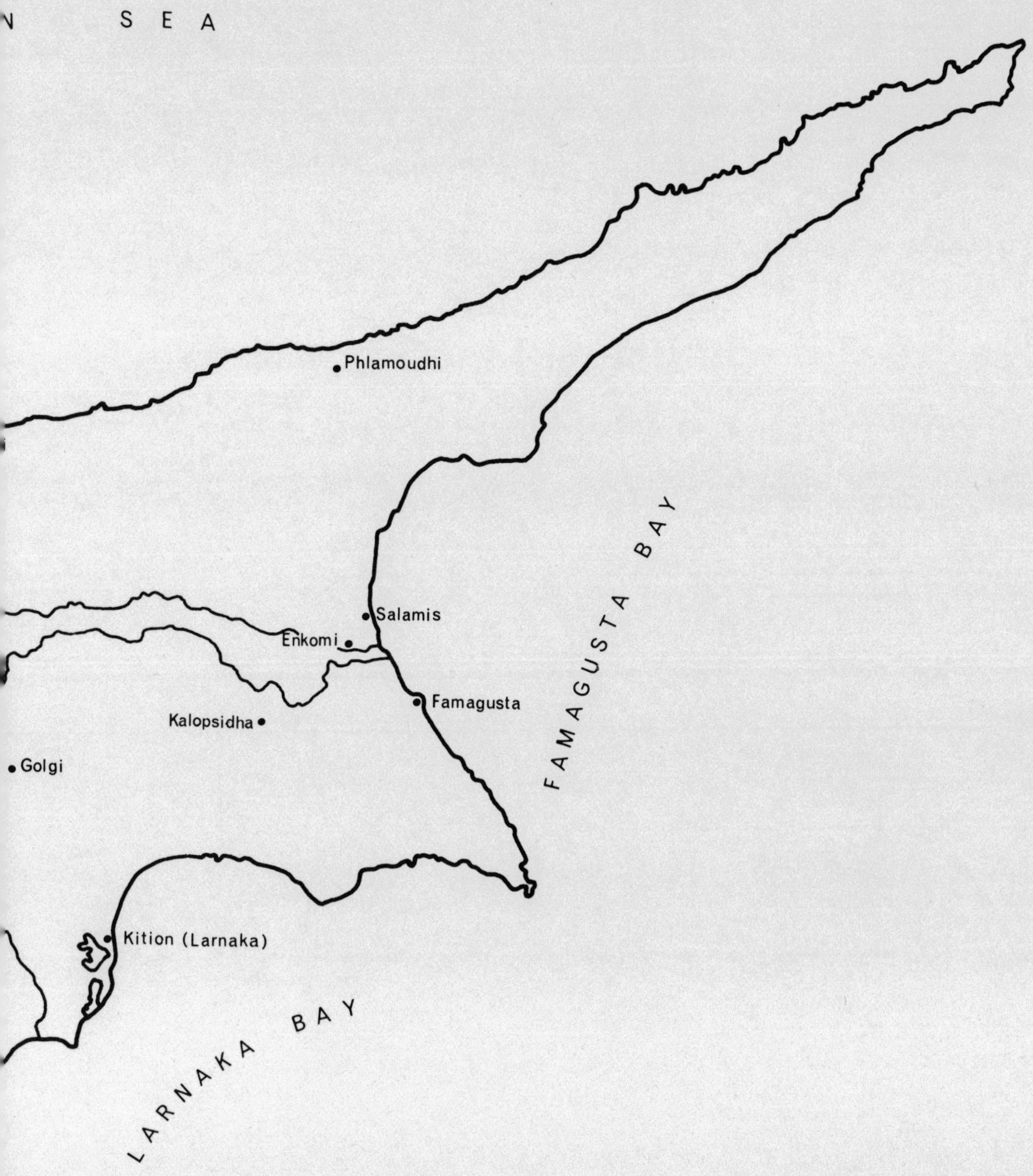

N   S E A

● Phlamoudhi

F A M A G U S T A   B A Y

● Salamis

Enkomi ●

● Famagusta

Kalopsidha ●

● Golgi

Kition (Larnaka)

L A R N A K A   B A Y

700–500	White-painted and red-bodied pottery; rectilinear and circle styles.
650–600	Closer commercial connections with Syria, Palestine, and Anatolia.
600–540	Egyptian control of Cyprus, with political conquest by Pharaoh Ahmose II (Amasis), 569 to 525.
540	Persian domination but Cyprus retains privileges of independence, as evidenced by issues of coinage by Euelthon, king of Salamis. / Free communications between Cyprus and Greece.
499	Collapse of Ionian Revolt (Ionia and Cyprus attempt to free themselves from Persian rule) briefly interrupts Hellenic-Cypriote connections. / Cyprus chief supply base for operations of Persian fleet in Aegean.

475–400 Classical Period I

470–450	Greeks attempt to liberate Cyprus from Persians. Athens withdraws fleet after Kimon's death at siege of Kition. Cypriote Greek cities cut off politically from mainland Greece but importation of pottery from Athens continues. / Persian domination continues.
425–332	Still subordinate to Persian rule, Greeks and Phoenicians contend for internal mastery of Cyprus. / Ascending throne of Salamis in 411, King Evagoras I, descendant of Teucer, works to unite Cyprus in an attempt to overthrow Persian domination. His army is defeated in 380, and Cyprus remains under Persian control.

400–325 Classical Period II

351–332	Pnytagoras, king of Salamis, and other city kings overthrow Persian rule and cooperate with Alexander the Great by supplying him with a fleet at siege of Tyre. / Alexander's conquests place Cyprus firmly in Greek world.
323	Alexander's death followed by political unrest. His successors, Ptolemy in Egypt and Antigonos in the East, contend for control of Cyprus.
310	Nikokreon, king of Salamis (331–310) and ally of Alexander, commits suicide on threat of death by Ptolemy. Great cenotaph with clay statues and other works of art created in Salamis necropolis.

325–58 Hellenistic Period

312	Ptolemy kills Pumiathon, last king of Kition (361–312), and destroys temple of Herakles-Melqart at Kition. / Marion, an old Greek city, destroyed and its population moved to Paphos.
306	Demetrios Poliorcetes defeats Ptolemy in naval battle off Salamis. Antigonos and son Demetrios rule Cyprus for twelve years.
295	Demetrios, busy in Greece, abandons Cyprus.
294	Ptolemy I conquers Cyprus, abolishes independent kingdoms, and makes coinage part of Ptolemaic system. Capital moved to Paphos.
285–246	Ptolemy II, Philadelphus. Ptolemaic dynastic cult established, reflected in votive sculpture. Marion refounded as Arsinoë (Aphrodite). / Zeno of Kition (336–264) founds universal philosophy, Stoicism.

246–221	Ptolemy III, Euergetes. Ptolemaic prosperity from Asia Minor to North Africa.
168	Antiochos IV Epiphanes of Syria attacks Cyprus, but Rome forces his withdrawal.
58	Cyprus ceded to Rome.

58 B.C.–A.D. 400 Graeco-Roman Period

52–51	Cicero, the Roman orator, institutes tax reforms as governor of Cilicia (and Cyprus).
47–30	Julius Caesar returns Cyprus to Egypt. After Battle of Actium and Cleopatra's death the island passes back to Imperial Rome.
31/27 B.C. –A.D. 14	Emperor Augustus. Cyprus becomes imperial province. After 22 B.C., Cyprus returned to the Senate, and Plautius, proconsul of Cyprus, strikes coins showing temple of Aphrodite at Paphos. Proconsuls rule from Paphos.
41–54	Emperor Claudius. *Koinon Kyprion* ("Federation of Cyprus") is responsible for bronze coinages.
45	Proconsul Sergius Paulus converted to Christianity by (Saints) Paul and Barnabas at Paphos.
69–79	Emperor Vespasian, conqueror of Jerusalem. In 76–77 a mint at Antioch-on-the-Orontes transferred to Cyprus, bringing economic relief after earthquake.
81–96	Emperor Domitian.
98–117	Emperor Trajan. / Restoration and rebuilding of damaged buildings at Salamis.
117–138	Emperor Hadrian. / Further rebuilding following Jewish uprising against Roman rule early in reign.
138–192	Antonine Emperors.
193–211	Emperor Septimius Severus' imposing bronze statue, in the heroic nude as Mars Pater, set up at the head of aqueduct to Salamis. (It is now in the Cyprus Museum.)
306–337	Emperor Constantine the Great embraces Christianity and (325) founds Constantinople.
327	Saint Helena, mother of Constantine, lands on Cyprus from Jerusalem with portions of the True Cross and the Cross of the Penitent Thief. She founds Monastery of Stavrovouni, and new churches and schools are established.
332 and 342	Severe earthquakes destroy Salamis Gymnasium. City rebuilt under Emperor Constantius II (337–361) and renamed Constantia. / Salamis-Constantia replaces Paphos as capital of Cyprus.
379–395	Emperor Theodosius I, last ruler of both Eastern and Western Empires, closes most pagan temples.

431 Council of Ephesos grants autonomy to Church of Cyprus.

647–648 Arab destruction leads to gradual abandonment of Salamis.

Pottery

Pottery Chronology

Early Cypriote

2300–1950 B.C.	I
1950–1925/1900	II
1925/1900–1875/1850	IIIA
1875/1850–1800	IIIB

Middle Cypriote

1800–1750	I
1750–1700	II
1700–1600	III

Late Cypriote

1600–1450	IA
1450–1400	IB
1400–1350	IIA
1350–1275	IIB
1275–1230	IIC
1230–1150	IIIA
1150–1050	IIIB

Cypro-geometric

1050–950	I
950–850	II
850–700	III

Cypro-archaic

700–600	I
600–475	II

Cypro-classical

475–400	I
400–325	II

1. Knob-Lug Bowl Black Polished Ware. Early Cypriote I – Middle Cypriote II. H. 0.057 m.; Diam.
0.105 m. (72.43). The surface luster is produced by polishing the surface with a smooth tool such as
a worn pebble or piece of bone. Essentially an early variety of Red Polished Ware, the black finish
is achieved by firing in a reduction atmosphere. The incised patterns are filled with a white chalky
matter.

2. Small Amphora with String-Hole Projections Red Polished III Ware. Early Cypriote III – Middle Cypriote II. From Alambra. H. 0.13 m.; Diam. 0.095 m. (72.28). The technique is identical to that of Black Polished Ware, except that the vessel is fired in an oxidizing atmosphere. The process is based on Anatolian pottery types, but the shapes, characterized by rounded bases, become a distinguishing feature of Cypriote wares.

3. Gourd Juglet Red Polished III Ware. Early Cypriote III–Middle Cypriote II. From Alambra. H. 0.18 m.; Diam. 0.111 m. (72.31). See no. 4 for discussion.

4. Gourd Juglet   Red Polished III Ware. Early Cypriote III – Middle Cypriote II. From Alambra. H. 0.15 m.; Diam. 0.101 m. (72.33). This type of vase, as indicated by its name, was derived from containers made of dried gourds that may also have been decorated with incised patterns. Nos. 3 and 4 show the variety of decoration possible within a simple technique.

5. Tripod Jug White Painted III–V String-hole Style. Middle Cypriote II–III. H. 0.195 m.; Diam. 0.108 m. (72.81). Painted rather than incised patterns decorate this type of jug, which is a modified version of a Red Polished Ware shape. The color reversal (to dark on a light ground) is reminiscent of earlier Chalcolithic pottery.

6. Ram-Shaped Vase White Painted V Ware. Middle Cypriote III. H. 0.161 m.; Diam. 0.203 m.
(72.132). From the Early Bronze Age on, vases in the shapes of animals, real or imaginary, are one
of the most appealing products of Cypriote art. This example seems to have been conceived as a
round-bodied spouted pitcher on three legs, the ram's head being attached as an afterthought.

7. Tankard White Slip I Ware. Late Cypriote I. H. 0.212 m.; Diam. 0.156 m. (72.86). See no. 8 for discussion.

8. Hemispherical Bowl White Slip I Ware. Late Cypriote I. H. 0.086 m.; Diam. 0.162 m. (72.87). White-Slip Ware was widely exported during the sixteenth century B.C. when copper mining became a thriving industry and the island prospered. So-called from the characteristic thick white slip applied on the dark-colored clay, it is one of the most typical Cypriote Late Bronze Age wares. The geometrical decoration in brown matte is imitative of stitching on leather prototypes. Vases of this kind, of which nos. 7 and 8 are examples, have been found on Rhodes, Thera, Crete, and in Syria, Palestine, and Egypt.

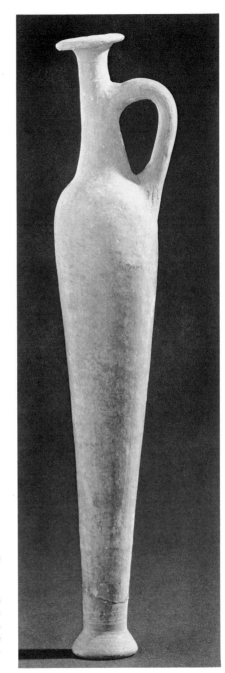

9. Spindle Bottle   Red Lustrous Wheel-made
Ware. Late Cypriote I. H. 0.32 m.; Diam. 0.057 m.
(72.5). The origin of this shape is clearly non-
Cypriote and was probably inspired by Syrian
vessels. Of the various bottle forms, this type is
the most popular, perhaps for the opium trade,
although fragile and seemingly impractical. The
luster is achieved by burnishing the slipped surface with a smooth tool.

11. Bowl Base-ring II Ware. Late Cypriote II–IIIA. H. 0.073 m.; Diam. 0.154 m. (Sarah Elizabeth Simpson Fund. 16.188). The outstanding feature of Base-ring Ware is the introduction of new shapes and white paint. Again, vessels of another material (see nos. 3-4), namely metal, prompt the manufacture of ceramic imitations. The thin walls, sharp profiles, ribbon handles, ridges around the neck (copying the metal rings used to join the handle to the neck), base rings, and dull or semilustrous surface of nos. 10 and 11 combine to produce a convincing effect.

10. Jug Base-ring II Ware. Late Cypriote II. H. 0.265 m.; Diam. 0.147 m. (Gift of Horace L. Mayer. 62.1186). See no. 11 for discussion.

12. Amphoroid Krater Cypro-Mycenaean Pictorial Style. Late Cypriote II. H. 0.436 m.; Diam. 0.355 m. (H. L. Pierce Fund. 01.8044). One new feature of the Late Cypriote II period is the abundance of Mycenaean style pottery. For large vases, this shape is perhaps the most favored in the fourteenth and early thirteenth centuries; the piriform body provides a large field for the new pictorial compositions. Chariot scenes such as this are one of the most popular subjects. The two figures in front of the horses, "roped" together, may be belt-wrestling.

13. Stirrup Jar Proto-White Painted Ware. Late Cypriote III. H. 0.155 m.; Diam. 0.126 m. (Sarah Elizabeth Simpson Fund. 16.190). See no. 14 for discussion.

14. Three-Handled Jar Proto-White Painted Ware. Late Cypriote III. H. 0.16 m.; Diam. 0.143 m. (72.94). Apart from imports from the Greek mainland and islands such as Rhodes, Mycenaean vases were made locally. The stirrup jar (no. 13), a Cypriote version of Mycenaean IIIC ware, has less spontaneous and balanced proportions than its stylistic models. The piriform three-handled jar (no. 14), also derived from the Mycenaean type, is decorated in typical hatched pattern and horizontal bands. Within the repertory, these two shapes were particularly favored by Cypriote potters.

15. Double Juglet with Joined Handle Base-ring I Ware. Late Cypriote I. H. 0.102 m. (Gift of Richard R. Wagner. 65.1172). Like animal shaped vases, composite vessels form an imaginative and lively type of Cypriote pottery. The clay is gray and fine bodied, fired hard to produce a light, somewhat lustrous body.

16. Bowl on Low Foot Bichrome III Ware. Cypro-geometric III. H. 0.092 m.; Diam. 0.137 m. (72.98). The well-defined shape of this bowl is an early form of the kylix, or two-handled drinking cup. The introduction of animals or birds within the paneled zones occurs in this period; on the example here, a long-necked prancing bird decorates each side. The inside of the bowl has narrow bands of black matte and wider bands of red.

17. Barrel-Shaped Jug Bichrome I Ware. Cypro-geometric I. H. 0.375 m.; W. 0.29 m. (Gift of Horace L. Mayer. 57.751). The Cypro-geometric style represents a development from Late Cypriote III prototypes; the shapes become more articulated and the designs more purely geometrical. Bichrome I is characterized by the additional use of red beside the black or brown matte painted on a light colored slip.

18. Small Handle-Ridge Jug   Black-on-Red I Ware. Cypro-geometric III. H. 0.091 m.;
Diam. 0.057 m. (72.61). This juglet is typical of this fabric and was produced in large
quantities. The pattern of concentric circles was achieved by means of a compass fitted
with a row of small brushes.

19. Spout-Jug   Black-on-Red II Ware. Cypro-archaic I. H. 0.09 m.; Diam. 0.067 m. (72.52).
See no. 20 for discussion.

20. Jug with Pinched Rim   White Painted IV Ware. Cypro-archaic I. H. 0.081 m.; Diam. 0.058 m. (72.60). The juglet with pointed spout and loop-handle (no. 19) represents the continued use of compass-drawn decorations, a form that occurs in other fabrics as well, such as no. 20, the White Painted jug. The combination of concentric circles and horizontal lines is a staple element within the repertory, developed from the earlier Geometric style.

21. Jar with Loop-Legs Bichrome IV Ware. Cypro-archaic I–II. H. 0.22 m.; Diam. 0.208 m. (H. L. Pierce Fund. 01.8047). This style represents the most typical production of Cypro-archaic pottery, and it is a welcome contrast to the prolific geometric patterns. The handles are transformed into animal heads, and the conventional bird with lotus flower is depicted in strong lines and sharp tones of black and red.

22. Jug Bichrome IV Ware. Cypro-archaic I–IIA. H. 0.299 m.; Diam. 0.199 m. (H. L. Pierce Fund. 01.8046). This low-slung jug with trefoil lip seems to be a variant of the free-field style, which is characterized by a single element, such as a bird, on the shoulder of the jug. Here, an especially inventive painter was not content with the predictable lotus flowers and birds. He has decorated the lower body with a fantastic two-headed winged creature apparently wearing helmets.

22a. Front view.

23. Jug with Modeled Bull Protome   Bichrome Red Ware II. Cypro-archaic II – Cypro-classical IA. H. 0.279 m.; Diam. 0.182 m. (H. L. Pierce Fund. 01.8045). A variation of the Black-on-Red II Ware, this style is distinguished by the use of white in addition to the black. The spout in the form of an animal head is also typical of this ware.

Terracottas

25. Goat Geometric. H. 0.134 m.; L. 0.092 m. (72.134). Mycenaean influence is evident in this terracotta goat, but the vigorous naturalistic style is characteristic of Cypriote artists. The goat is solid and hand modeled, and red and black paint is used for details and designs. Figurines such as this one were placed in tombs to replace sacrificed animals in the Late Bronze and Early Iron Ages.

24. Female Figurine Base-ring Ware. Late Cypriote II. H. 0.111 m. (72.154). The statuette is hand modeled in a frontal position with her hands at her breasts. Her head is triangular and flat on top. An incised triangle marks her abdomen. Traces of red and black paint are found on her abdomen and on the features of her face; painted stripes are visible on her neck and the shoulder area. This type of female idol was common in Late Bronze Age tombs with Mycenaean contacts and was significant in funerary practices.

26. Horse with Rider   Archaic. H. 0.225 m.; L. 0.101 m. (72.140). The horse and rider are hand modeled from brown terracotta with red and matte black paint used for details. The horse is modeled in the conventional shape of a small body with a long neck and a high crested mane. The rider, modeled separately and then added to the horse's back, is legless. Horsemen of this type are votary figures, dedicated to Apollo or to the god of the regional cult.

27. Man with Tympanum Archaic. H. 0.14 m. (72.150). The lower part of the body is handmade and cylindrical, probably shaped to represent a chiton. The man wears a headdress (a fillet) of a type popular in the sixth century B.C. Traces of white slip are visible, and red paint is used for details. The tympanum held by this votary and the musical instruments played by similar figurines indicate that music was used in cult rituals.

28. Votary Figurine   Archaic.
H. 0.105 m. (72.147).

29. Votary Figurine   Archaic.
H. 0.086 m. (72.146).

28–30. The two solid votary figures (nos. 28 and 29) are hand modeled in buff terracotta, and the details are painted in black and red. No. 28, wearing a small pointed cap, is in a conventional pose of adoration; the left hand at his mouth and the right arm across his body. The method of production was the "snowman" technique, which was not associated with the potters' trade, as was the production of earlier, hollow figurines. No. 29 is an unusual example of a votary holding a human mask over his face. The votary's mask is very similar to no. 30: the eyes are not modeled plastically but are drawn in black paint, which is also used for the beard and eyebrows. The mouth, ears, and circles on the cheeks are painted in red, and forehead studs are present on both masks. The hair of no. 29 falls down his back in two plaits. He appears to be holding a dagger in his right hand.

30. Painted Terracotta Mask   Archaic. H. 0.105 m. (72.161).

31. Female Idol Archaic. H. 0.118 m. (72.155). The statuette is moulded with an unfinished back. She is either nude or wearing a transparent tunic; she is adorned with an elaborate headdress, bracelet and a necklace of rosettes and a pendant. The style and moulded technique are probably of Syrian origin. Statuettes of this type are associated with the cult of Golgia, a goddess equated with Aphrodite, and were doubtless representations of the goddess herself.

32. Woman Holding Child Archaic. H. 0.178 m. (72.158). The statuette is moulded in an upright frontal position. The woman has a broad face, and her hair is pulled behind her ears and then combed forward into two plaits. She wears a short himation over a long tunic and holds a child that suckles her breast. Eastern influence is apparent in the shape of the woman's head, her short neck, and the features of her face; and the statuette is an example of the Daedalic style. The woman represented is probably Aphrodite. The statuette was formed by pressing clay into a shallow mould of the woman's body and then scraping off the excess clay, leaving an unfinished back. No handmade details are added.

Sculpture

33. Head of a Man in a Near Eastern Helmet Light stone. Archaic. H. 0.175 m. (72.340). The helmet has a large top piece and cheek flaps of proportionate size, which are turned up against the sides. The hair is caught up into a series of braids, contained in a cloth on the back of the neck.

34. Head of a Man in an Eastern Helmet   Light stone. Archaic. H. 0.302 m. (72.320). The man wears a cloth liner under his helmet. The side flaps are turned up, and the hair behind is contained in a large cloth that allows it to flare out at the sides. He is the so-called Phoenician Votary, Type 8 in the British Museum classification of Cypriote sculpture.

35. Head of a Man in a Headcloth   Dark stone. Archaic. H. 0.137 m. (72.318). The headdress is arranged in a vaguely Egyptian style. There is a pattern of rectangles and zigzags on the cloth, which covers the entire head and contains the hair on the back of the neck. There are double-spiral earrings on the ears.

36. Musician Playing Double Flutes   Light brown stone. Archaic. H. 0.191 m. (72.317).
This half-figure, from a small statue, wears an Egyptian headcloth and a long tunic with
short sleeves. He was doubtless making music at a banquet, at funeral rites, or in the
precinct of a temple.

37. Man in Near Eastern Dress Light stone. Archaic. H. 0.327 m. (72.311). The man wears a long tunic with short sleeves and a mantle that covers both shoulders and his right side. He holds his right arm as if it were in a sling; his left arm is held tightly against his side. His bare feet are planted firmly, side by side, on the small rectangular plinth. The forms of the body match the flatness of the drapery.

38. Male Votary Light stone. Archaic. H. 0.175 m. (72.350). The figure holds an object, like a rectangular tablet, in his right hand, against the long tunic. The garment and forms of the body are so simply conceived that it is difficult to tell whether an overmantle is represented. It may have been shown in paint. The hair is arranged in the series of curls over the forehead and wavy lines behind, characteristic of nude *Kouroi* ("Apollos") from Cyprus and Naukratis.

39. A God, Hero, or Votary   Light stone. Archaic. H. 0.267 m. (72.322). A flat fillet encircles the brow of this head, the tassels of one or both ends hanging down on a line with the nose, amid the locks enframing the forehead. Above and behind the fillet is a cloth cap (?), in a series of layers that are divided up into rectangular patterns. A row of curls, directly above the fillet, extends into the temples in front of the ears. The beard is represented by tight curls that echo those on the head. This head, in the best Cypriote Late Archaic style, ought to represent a mythological figure of note.

40. Priest or Votary Light stone. Archaic–Classical. H. 0.305 m. (72.326). The Jovian locks of this head are encircled by a large wreath. The beard is arranged in Archaic curls, in contrast to the freedom and imagination of the hair around the forehead, on the back of the head at the start of the neck, and on the crown of the head.

41. Priest or Votary   Light stone. Archaic–Classical. H. 0.286 m. (72.325). The face, hair, and beard of this head have an almost Pheidian look, although in terms of lingering Archaism. An unusual wreath encircles the brow, and extra ivy leaves lie on the hair above the forehead. The beard is modern in fifth century terms, just below the cheeks and around the mouth. At the sides and in front of the neck, the curls follow the Archaic tradition.

42. Priest or Votary   Dark stone. Archaic–Classical. H. 0.273 m. (72.324). Despite
the damage brought about by wear and water, this head has considerable individu-
ality. The condition of the ears and the right eye suggest the statue may have been
left unfinished.

43. Goddess or Votary Light stone. Archaic, ca. 500 B.C. H. 0.162 m. (72.152). The figure wears a Near Eastern headcloth that contains her hair as it falls down her back. She has a large necklace, and her right hand is raised to hold a bird, flower, pomegranate, or a large pendant in the center of the necklace. Her long tunic or chiton is covered by a thin himation with folds lightly expressed by incision, which follows the Archaic Ionian fashion. Traces of color remain throughout. Her feet are together on a small, rectangular plinth, and they appear to be covered by shoes or slippers. Her left hand is at her side and holds a small, uncertain object. She is a good, typical example of the mixed Near Eastern and Attic Ionian styles as reflected in Cypriote sculpture.

44. Goddess or Woman Nursing a Baby Light stone. Archaic. H. 0.102 m. (72.306). The figure, seated frontally on a high-backed throne with heavy arms, holds a child across her lap. She wears a long garment and a necklace. Her feet are bare. The child suckles her left breast. There are traces of pink color.

45. Youth Wearing a Phrygian Cap Light brown stone. Hellenistic or Graeco-Roman. H. 0.121 m. (72.341). A series of stylized curls enframes the forehead of this head in a semicircle, running down in front of the ears under the cap at the sides. The eyes were finished in paint, and there are traces of red on the lips.

46. Berenike II, Wife of Ptolemy III (246–221 B.C.)   Light stone. Hellenistic (or later?). H. 0.127 m. (72.329). Berenike wears her himation drawn up as a veil over her head, in the manner of a Hellenistic queen. It fits closely to her head, leaving only the hair over her forehead exposed. This hair is drawn back in tight groups of strands or waves, almost resembling a "melon" hair style. The lady is identified on the basis of coins, being Berenike Ptolemy III's wife rather than his grandmother, Berenike I, wife of Ptolemy I Soter.

47. Head of a Ptolemaic King or Official, perhaps Ptolemy III Euergetes (246 to 221 B.C.)ʳ Light stone. Hellenistic. H. 0.331 m. (72.336). The hair is unusually well modeled, being combed forward in the manner of Macedonian kings. He wears a precisely carved garland of laurel leaves on his head. The strong Skopasian, or Pergamene, turn of the head and neck belongs to Hellenistic portraiture from about 250 to 50 B.C. An identification as Ptolemy III seems plausible, for this head in profile catches something of his plumpness below the chin.

48. Priest or Votary   Light stone. Graeco-Roman. H. 0.102 m. (72.347). He wears a diadem, which might suggest he belongs to the Ptolemaic or Roman ruling classes. The head does not, however, appear to be a portrait of a known person.

49. Head of Emperor Augustus (27 B.C.–A.D. 14)   Dark stone. Graeco-Roman. H. 0.325 m. (Gift of Jerome M. Eisenberg and Frederick Richman. 1971.325). The head, in profile to the left, is from a high relief. The emperor wears a laurel wreath. He was probably shown in civic garb in a himation or possibly a toga, in an allegorical scene such as reception by a city-Tyche (Goddess of Fortune, possibly representing Salamis)—or in a grouping with one or more local magistrates. Such reliefs are known from the Greek imperial world, but they are very rare. This is the only surviving portrait of Augustus in Cypriote limestone and one of the few imperial portraits in Cypriote stone which resembles its subject in a standard East Greek pan-Mediterranean sense.

Coins

50. Silver Stater Struck at Lapethos Ca. 440–400 B.C. Diam. 23 mm. (Theodora Wilbour Fund in Memory of Zoë Wilbour. 58.515). Athena on the obverse wears an earring and a Corinthian helmet decorated with a lotus flower design. On the reverse, a bearded head of Herakles wearing a lion's skin faces right. (From the Celenderis hoard.)

51. Silver Stater of Baalmelek II (King of Kition and Idalion) 425–400 B.C. Diam. 24 mm. (H. L. Pierce Fund. 04.1154). The obverse (not illustrated), struck from a very worn die, shows Herakles striding to the right, holding his club and a bow. On the reverse, within a square incuse, a lion pulls down a stag. The Phoenician inscription above the animals designates the king in whose reign the stater was minted. (From the E. P. Warren collection.)

52. Silver Stater of Evagoras I (King of Salamis) 411–373 B.C. Diam. 21 mm. (H. L. Pierce Fund. 04.1158). See no. 53 for discussion.

53. Silver Stater of Evagoras I (King of Salamis) 411–373 B.C. Diam. 23 mm. (Theodora Wilbour Fund in Memory of Zoë Wilbour. 59.1). On obverse of no. 52 a head of Herakles wearing a lion's skin faces to the right. On obverse of no. 53, Herakles, holding a rhyton in his left hand and a club in his right, is seated facing to the right on a lion's skin placed over a rock. On both reverses, a goat lies with legs folded on a dotted ground line (reverse of no. 52 not illustrated). The name of Evagoras appears, on both coins, in Cypriote letters on the obverse and in abbreviated form on the reverse, in a mixture of Cypriote and Greek, where he is described as king. (No. 52 is from the E. P. Warren collection.)

50a. Obverse.

52a. Obverse.

50b. Reverse.

53a. Reverse.

51a. Reverse.

53b. Obverse.

54a. Obverse.

54b. Reverse.

55a. Reverse.

54. Gold Stater of Nikokreon (King of Salamis) 331–310 B.C. Diam. 17 mm. (Theodora Wilbour Fund in Memory of Zoë Wilbour. 49.1905). The bust of Aphrodite on the obverse is ornamented with earrings, a necklace, and a crown made of a band attached to four semioval plates on the side of her head. The Aphrodite on the reverse appears as a city-goddess wearing earrings, necklace, and an elaborately turreted crown.

55. Greek Imperial Silver Tetradrachm Struck in Cyprus in A.D. 77–78 during reign of Vespasian (A.D. 69 –79) Diam. 25.5 mm. (Theodora Wilbour Fund in Memory of Zoë Wilbour. 60.1435). On the obverse (not illustrated) a laureate bust of the emperor faces left. The temple of Aphrodite at Paphos is shown on the reverse, cross-beams joining the central columns with a low roofed wing on either side. The sacred cone here appears to fill the central area of the temple.

56a. Obverse.

56. Greek Imperial Bronze Coin   Struck in Cyprus in A.D. 76–77 during the reign of Vespasian (A.D. 69–79). Diam. 27 mm. (Gift of Mr. and Mrs. Cornelius C. Vermeule III. 67.901). A laureate bust of Emperor Vespasian faces right on the obverse On the reverse (not illustrated) Zeus stands holding a phiale in his right hand and a scepter in his left. An eagle perches on his left arm. (From the Duke of Argyll Collection.)

57. Greek Imperial Bronze Coin   Struck in Cyprus during the reign of Antoninus Pius (A.D. 138–161). Diam. 33 mm. (Gift of Mr. and Mrs. Cornelius C. Vermeule III. 67.902). The obverse portrait (not illustrated) is a laureate bust of the emperor facing to the right. On the reverse, his successor, Marcus Aurelius, wearing drapery and a cuirass, faces to the right. (From the Duke of Argyll Collection.)

57a. Reverse.

58a. Obverse.   **58b.** Reverse.

58. Greek Imperial Bronze Coin   Struck in Cyprus in
A.D. 206–207 during the reign of Septimius Severus
(A.D. 193–211). Diam. 33.5 mm. (Theodora Wilbour Fund
in Memory of Zoë Wilbour. 63.423). On the obverse the
emperor faces right wearing a laurel wreath, drapery,
and a cuirass. The temple of Aphrodite at Paphos on
the reverse has a semicircular forecourt enclosed by a
latticework fence with open gates. Above the wings on
each side of the building a bird faces outward. A cres-
cent appears above the central section of the roof. On
this coin the sacred cone has a double flat top.

Selected Bibliography

(Many of the books listed below contain detailed bibliographies for the specialist.)

Ashmole, B. "Cyprus." In *The Ancient World,* edited by H. A. Groenewegen-Frankfort and B. Ashmole. The Library of Art History. Vol. 1, pp. 251–253. New York, 1967. (1000 to 58 B.C.)

Åström, P. *The Middle Cypriote Bronze Age.* Lund, 1957.

—— *Who's Who in Cypriote Archaeology: Biographical and Bibliographical Notes.* Studies in Mediterranean Archaeology. Vol. 23. Göteborg, 1971. (The listings contain the writings of all scholars working in Cypriote archaeology.)

Catling, H. W. "Cyprus in the Neolithic and Chalcolithic Periods." In *The Cambridge Ancient History,* 3rd ed. Vol. 1. Cambridge, 1970.

—— "Cyprus in the Early Bronze Age." In *The Cambridge Ancient History,* 3rd ed. Vol. 1. Cambridge, 1971.

Cesnola, L. P. di *A Descriptive Atlas of the Cesnola Collection of Cypriote Antiquities in the Metropolitan Museum of Art, New York.* 3 vols. Boston, 1885–1903.

—— *Cyprus: Its Ancient Cities, Tombs, and Temples.* New York, 1878.

Comstock, M. B., and Vermeule, C. C. *Greek, Etruscan & Roman Art: The Classical Collections of the Museum of Fine Arts.* Boston, 1972.

—— *Greek, Etruscan & Roman Bronzes in the Museum of Fine Arts, Boston.* Boston, 1971. (Cypriote jewelry, pp. 188–198; Cypriote tools, weapons, armor, instruments, pp. 392–403.)

"Cyprus." In *Nagel's Encyclopedia Guide.* Geneva, 1969.

Cyprus at the Dawn of Her History: From the Neolithic to the Bronze Age — Archaeologia Viva. The Collections of the Cyprus Museum. Vol. 2, no. 3, March–May 1969. (Articles by ten famous scholars of Cypriote archaeology, on migrations, settlements, economy, industry, art, seals, and writing.)

Dikaios, P. *A Guide to the Cyprus Museum.* 3rd rev. ed. Nicosia, 1961.

Gunnis, R. *Historic Cyprus: A Guide to Its Towns and Villages, Monasteries and Castles.* London, 1936. 2nd ed. London, 1947.

Hill, G. F. (later Sir George). *A Catalogue of the Greek Coins in the British Museum: Catalogue of the Greek Coins of Cyprus.* London, 1904.

Hill, Sir George. *A History of Cyprus: To the Conquest by Richard Lion Heart.* Vol. 1. Cambridge, 1940.

Karageorghis, V. *Cyprus.* Geneva and London, 1969.

—— *Mycenaean Art from Cyprus.* Nicosia, 1968.

—— *Salamis in Cyprus: Homeric, Hellenistic, and Roman.* London, 1969.

—— *Treasures in the Cyprus Museum.* Nicosia, 1962.

Leipen, N. *The Loch Collection of Cypriote Antiquities: Lionel Massey Memorial Exhibition.* Toronto: Royal Ontario Museum, 1966.

McFadden, E. *The Glitter and the Gold: A Spirited Account of the Metropolitan Museum of Art's First Director, the Audacious and High-handed Luigi Palma di Cesnola.* New York, 1971.

Merrillees, R. S. *The Cypriote Bronze Age Pottery Found in Egypt.* Studies in Mediterranean Archaeology. Vol. 18. Lund, 1968.

Myres, John L. *Handbook of the Cesnola Collection of Antiquities from Cyprus.* New York: The Metropolitan Museum of Art, 1914.

Nicolaou, K. *Ancient Monuments of Cyprus.* Nicosia, 1968.

Pierides, A. G. *Jewellery in the Cyprus Museum.* Nicosia, 1971.

Pryce, F. N. "Cypriote and Etruscan Sculpture." In *Catalogue of Sculpture in the Department of Greek and Roman Antiquities of the British Museum.* Vol. 1, part 2. London, 1931.

Richter, G. M. A. *Antiquities from the Island of Cyprus: Gift of Samuel P. Avery, Wadsworth Atheneum, Morgan Memorial.* Hartford, 1916.

Sjöqvist, E. *The Swedish Cyprus Expedition: Problems of the Late Cypriote Bronze Age.* Stockholm, 1940.

The Swedish Cyprus Expedition: Finds and Results of the Excavations in Cyprus, 1927–1931. Stockholm, 1934–.

Thurston, H. *Travellers' Guide: Cyprus.* New York, 1971.

Trendall, A. D., et al. *Handbook to the Nicholson Museum.* 2nd ed. Sydney, Australia, 1948.

Young, J. H., and Young, S. H. *Terracotta Figurines from Kourion in Cyprus.* Philadelphia: The University Museum, 1955.